YOUR KNOWLEDGE HAS VALUE

Emotion Artificial Intelligence as improvement for e-Learning during COVID-19

Hari K. C.

Bibliographic information published by the German National Library:

The German National Library lists this publication in the National Bibliography; detailed bibliographic data are available on the Internet at http://dnb.dnb.de.

ISBN: 9783346260338
This book is also available as an ebook.

© GRIN Publishing GmbH
Nymphenburger Straße 86
80636 München

Print and binding: Books on Demand GmbH, Norderstedt, Germany
Printed on acid-free paper from responsible sources.

The present work has been carefully prepared. Nevertheless, authors and publishers do not incur liability for the correctness of information, notes, links and advice as well as any printing errors.

GRIN web shop: https://www.grin.com/document/933196

Emotion Artificial Intelligence as improvement for e - Learning during COVID-19

By Er. Hari K.C.

Pashchimanchal Campus, Institute of Engineering

Tribhuvan University

Er. Hari K.C.

M.Sc. in Communication and Knowledge Engineering

Specialties in Machine learning, social network analysis, Neural network, AI, Data mining, IOT.

Eight years of experience in research and teaching. Act as Reviewers and board member in different international journals. Achieve Gold Medal award for best student during master study. Published various research papers in national and international journals.

ABSTRACT

Emotion Artificial Intelligence is one of the trending topics nowadays. It mainly deals with emotion recognition to determine the various emotions and behaviors of an individual. The number of researches is being carried out in emotion artificial intelligence to identify the various applications in real environment. The emotions of students are a key factor to determine the effective involvement of students in virtual learning. Due to the pandemic COVID -19, it is not possible for the Universities to conduct the physical classes. The Universities are taking the virtual classes, providing e - learning environment to the students to manage the academic sessions. The main idea of this paper is to improve and enhance the quality of e – learning by detecting and monitoring the emotions of students and provide quick response. The emotions of students such as excitement, happiness, confusion, sadness, desire and surprise are evaluated in this paper. Similarly, the movement of head, eye and whole face are also considered in this research. Different techniques such as concentration level measurement and artificial neural network are employed to identify the learner's involvement and their interest in attending e -learning classes. Finally, the emotion artificial Intelligence system will provide the feedback to the teacher to improve the learning environment. The system is tested with the bachelor level students of Pashchimanchal Campus.

Keywords: Artificial Intelligence, Neural network, e-learning, covid-19, emotion, University

ACKNOWLEDGEMENT

I am very thankful to Pashchimanchal Campus, Institute of Engineering for providing me the platform to perform this research.

I am grateful to all the students and colleagues who directly and indirectly help me for this.

TABLE OF CONTENTS

LIST OF FIGURES

LIST OF TABLES

INTRODUCTION

Due to the pandemic situation of COVID -19, the whole world is suffering and everything has been shut down to control the spread of corona virus. Industries, Automobiles, Universities, Service sectors etc. are closed however, the patients of COVID -19 positive are continuously increasing. Nepal is also suffering from this pandemic situation. According to the Ministry of Health and Population, the total cases of COVID -19 are 48138, the total infected are 14686, and recovered cases are 32964. Total death till now due to COVID -19 are 306 [6]. The government of Nepal is taking various actions such as Lockdown, employing frontline health workers, distributing masks, sanitizers to the needed individuals, disseminating COVID-19 preventive information's. The people are also taking precautions such as distancing to avoid such circumstances. Only the emergency tasks are going on and other tasks are pending due to this pandemic. The education sector is also suffering a lot therefore it is very difficult to manage the academic sessions by Ministry of Education, Science and Technology. There are total ten Universities in Nepal [9]. Tribhuvan University is the oldest and largest public University of Nepal. There are at least 3000 undergraduate programs and 2000 graduate programs run by different constituent and affiliated campuses all over the country. In this pandemic situation, Tribhuvan University as well as other Universities are also conducting the online classes to manage the academic sessions. Pashchimanchal Campus, Institute of Engineering is one of the institutes under Tribhuvan University.

Pashchimanchal Campus started the e- learning classes after the six month of long pandemic situation dated August 17, 2020. Teachers, students and all the related personnel are very motivated to continue the academic session after long time. However, the challenges are still there for all the campuses to continue the e- learning classes. Some of the challenges are slow internet problems, lack of internet in remote places, unavailability of digital devices, knowledge of operating digital devices, e-learning platforms and software's. After the survey conducted by Institute of Engineering, Tribhuvan University, it found that almost 50 percent of students are ready for online classes. Similarly, the internet service providers are providing student internet package at cheap prices. The e-learning process is going well in most cases but the next challenge for the campus is to improve the quality of e-learning so that the student's effectiveness can be seen in attending the classes until COVID -19 ends. This may take 1-2 years to control this pandemic as recently there are no vaccines available and many countries are involving in research to develop the effective vaccine [11]. E- learning provide the platform to the students for continuing the classes. Since the teachers doesn't see the students physically, it is very difficult for the teachers to grab the attention of the students in the online classes. The online classes need to be interactive to engage the students.

In this paper, for analyzing the student's emotions such as excitement, happiness, confusion, sadness, desire and surprise, the neural network model is designed to capture the facial expression. Deep learning is the emerging techniques to process large datasets of images with Kera's using TensorFlow backend. Convolution Neural Network is an artificial neural network that has specialization in detection and classification. Convolution neural network has hidden layers called convolution layers. This layer consists of neurons. Facial emotion recognition usually employs a training and testing stage to produce the desirable output [2]. The emotion of the students plays the vital role to determine the student interest in attending classes. Facial expressions are among the most universal forms of body language. The facial expressions are almost similar throughout the world. The facial expression, movement of head, eye, mouth helps to identify the emotions of the students so that the level of interest of student can be predicted form the emotion analysis of students. For example: A smile can be used to indicate happiness. Facial expression reveals the true feelings about a situation. Then, after collecting those information, e-learning quality can be improved and enhanced. The reaction of the students is analyzed during the teaching and learning course. Thus, the mood of students can be predicted easily which help to improve the e - learning environment. The feedback will be provided to teachers to enhance the teaching and learning process in e-learning.

OBJECTIVES

The objectives of this research are:

a) To design the convolution neural architecture for emotion identification.

b) To analyze the emotions to predict the mood of students.

c) To enhance the e-learning environment based on concentration level and feedback.

RELATED WORK

The study of facial expressions was started date back to early of 4th century BC. By the late 1980, cheap computing power s become available. This led to the development of robust face detection and face tracking algorithms. Then in, 19th century, the important work on facial expression analysis that has a relation to the modern-day science of automatic facial emotion recognition was the work done by Charles Darwin [2] In 21st century, various researchers' study about facial emotions and its applications using artificial intelligence. Similarly, other researches had been carried out in the field of e-learning. This research paper focus on combining both the e-learning and emotion recognition to predict the emotional state of the students in e-learning environment.

This paper [3] explains the effectiveness of e-learning measures, learning outcome and benefit of quality feedback on the effectiveness of e-learning solution. Different e-learning solutions and process are also considered in this paper. In paper [7], the authors describe the scope and applications of e-learning. Also, the author suggests a set of critical success factor and framework for developing e-learning environment. In this research paper [4], the researcher supports the emotional side of learners to raise the awareness and motivation. The importance of facial expression during educational game is also considered in this research with accuracy of 97 percent. Further, A pilot study is conducted using Machine learning concepts for emotion recognition on E learning community. The emotions are recognized from the speech of a person, textual sentiments given in social media and facial expression during study. The emotions are used to identify like and dislike of the learners [12]. The author in this paper [2] , explain the deep learning model to classify the various emotions of the human faces using three convolution layers. The accuracy of the model is 98 percent when working with FER2013 datasets.

Similarly, the researchers in this research paper [8], applies the support vector machine and K nearest neighbor algorithm to learn the emotional state based on facial expressions. Researcher proposed the hybrid information system combining computer vision and machine learning technology for visual and interactive e-learning system. The research motivates the educator to concern about the education of the learners by taking the feedback from the information system.

METHODOLOGY

A) System Architecture

System Architecture define the overall procedure and working of the emotion AI learning system. The main blocks in architecture are image preprocessing, feature engineering, concentration level metrics, convolution neural network, classification of emotions and feedback to teacher. From the video of student learning in online classes, the picture frames are collected at different time interval. Facial images are focused. Emotions and concentration level are classified at the final stage.

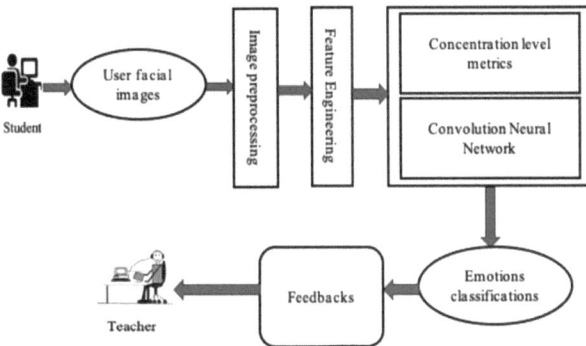

Figure1 : Block diagram of emotion AI learning system

The emotion AI learning system consist of student's facial image as input. Convolution Neural network is applied to the images using different hidden layers. Training dataset of images are used to train the images. Different concentration level is also measured such as high-level concentration, and low-level concentration. Then, emotions of student are obtained. The emotions may be excitement, happiness, confusion, sadness, desire and surprise. On the basis of these emotions and concentration level, the feedback is collected and provided to the teacher.

B) Algorithm

1) Start
2) Input students' images dataset.
3) Perform Preprocessing of images such as identifying facial key points, enhancement of image and cropping of images.

12

4) Perform feature engineering such as image segmentation, localization and features development.

5) Collecting Training set of data and testing set of data.

6) Convolution Neural network is trained using training set of data.

7) Measure student level of concentration.

8) Classify mood of student (excitement, happiness, confusion, sadness, desire and surprise) using testing images dataset of students

9) Obtain the feedback from the information collected from emotion and level of concentration.

10) Provide feedback to the teacher.

11) Stop

C) Image Preprocessing

After the image is inputted to the system, the first step in system is preprocessing of images. The face of the student is detected, then facial key points are obtained. Facial key points are also called Facial landmarks which generally specify the areas of the nose, eyes, mouth, etc. on the face, classified by 68 key points, with coordinates (x, y), for that face[5]. Image enhancement improve the performance of system. The noises in images are removed in this stage. Then, the image is cropped for the suitable region of image to include as the final input image.

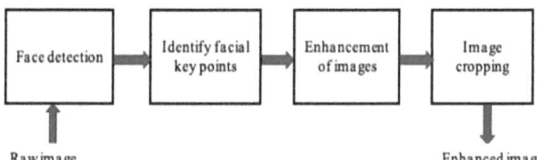

Figure2 : Image Preprocessing

D) Feature Engineering

In feature engineering, image segmentation, localization and feature generation are performed sequentially. The first step is image segmentation, which is used for contour detection or segments the multiple objects in a single image so that the classifier can quickly detect the faces in the picture. Face Localization detects the location and size of faces. Then finally, the feature variable is defined.

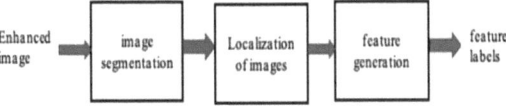

Figure3: Feature engineering

E) Concentration level measurement

Concentration level is measured by monitoring the head and eye movement. Eye detection is the important criteria for finding whether student is interested in topic or not [1]. Rotation of head is also the judging criteria for concentration level. For this, different frame of the video in different time intervals are taken for this purpose. Eye status can be recognized from the extracted eye region.

Head position can be detected by extracting the head region and determine whether the head is rotated or not. For high concentration level, the eyes and head should be in right position and in center. if the eyes are closed, it means the student is not focusing in the screen which indicate that the student has low concentration. The value 1 or 0 is allocated for eye and head position to determine concentration level. The value 1 indicate high level concentration and the value 0 indicate low level concentration.

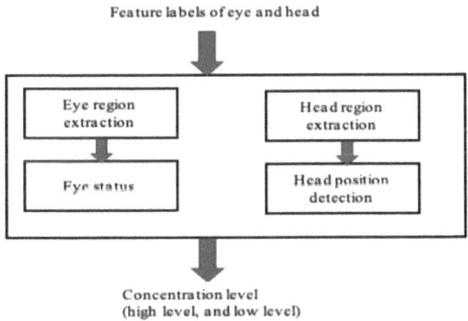

Figure4: Concentration level Measurement

F) Design of Convolution Neural network

A Convolution Neural network is designed with 3 convolution layers, three pooling layers, and two fully connected layers.

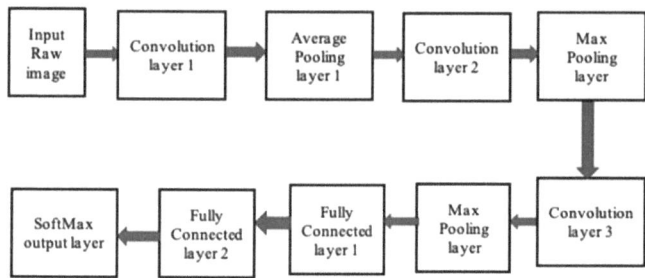

Figure5: Design of Convolution layer for emotion AI system

The parameters of Neural Network are as follows:

Table1: Parameters of Neural network

Stages	Parameters
Convolution layer 1	5*5
Convolution layer 2	4*4
Convolution layer 3	5*5
Max Pooling layer	3*3
Average Pooling layer	3*3
Fully Connected layer	7

DATA COLLECTION

Data are divided into two types. One is training set of data and other is testing set of data. The training set of data is obtained from Kaggle website and testing data images are collected from the e- learning class videos frame taken in Pashchimanchal campus, IOE, Tribhuvan University. The images are randomly collected from the online classes from webcam for testing purpose.

RESULT AND ANALYSIS

A) Face detection sample output

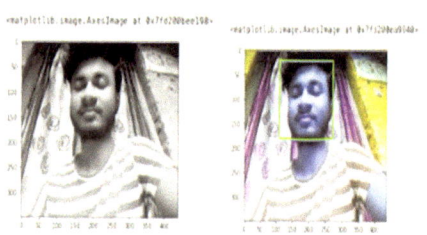

Figure6: Student 1face detection

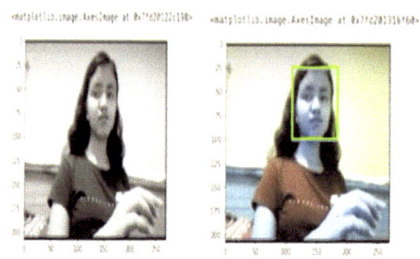

Figure7: Student 2 face detection

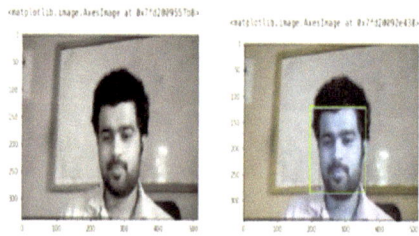

Figure8 : Student 3 face detection

B) Facial key points identification

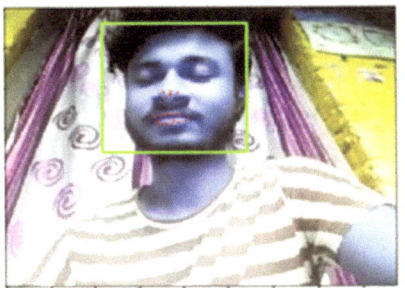

Figure9: Student 1 facial key points

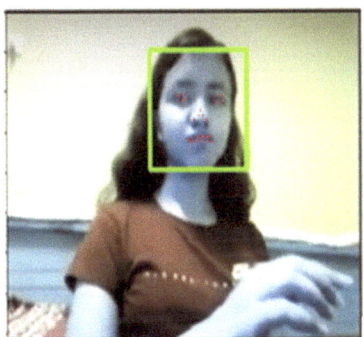

Figure10: Student 2 facial key points

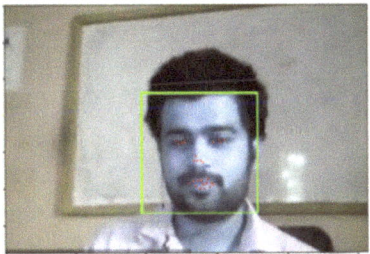

Figure11: Student 3 facial key points

C) Concentration level
1) Head movement

Table2: Head Movement

Head position of student / value	in frame	in center	Remarks
student 1	1	0	0.5
student 2	1	1	1
student 3	1	1	1

2) Eye

Table3: Eye Visibility

Eye	left eye visible	right eye visible	Remarks
student 1	0	0	0
student 2	1	1	1
student 3	1	1	1

3) Concentration level

Table4: Concentration level

Sample Student	head movement	Eye	Concentration level
student 1	0.5	0	0.5 (low concentration)
student 2	1	1	1 (high concentration)
student 3	1	1	1 (high concentration)

D) Emotion Classification
1) Student 1 Emotion

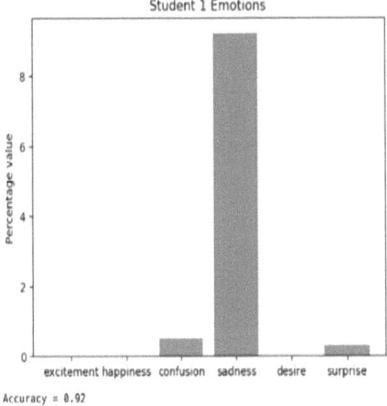

Figure12: Emotion Graph for Student 1

2) Student 2 Emotion

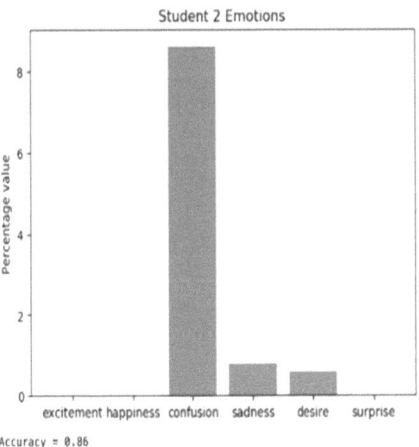

Figure13: Emotion Graph for Student 2

3) Student 3 Emotion

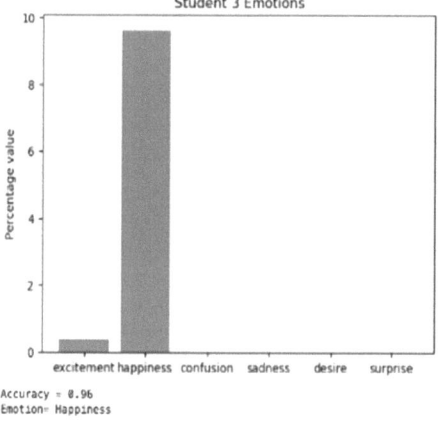

Accuracy = 0.96
Emotion= Happiness

Figure14: Emotion Graph for Student 3

E) Analysis

Table5: Analysis table

Sample Students	Emotion Class	Concentration Level	Feedback
1) Student 1	sadness	low level	not interested
2) Student 2	confusion	high level	interested but not understanding contents
3) Student 3	happiness	high level	interested and understanding contents

CONCLUSION

Finally, it has been concluded that emotion AI learning system is very useful in measuring the concentration level and emotions of the students taking online classes. Convolution Neural network gives the good overall accuracy for classifying the emotions. The face of students is properly detected and facial key points are determined which makes the classification of emotion much better. Thus, e-learning quality can be enhanced by taking the feedback given by the system. If the feedback is properly followed, the e-learning teaching and learning process will be improved during this COVID-19 pandemic.

REFERENCES

[1] Krithika. L.B., Laxmi Priya GG., Student Emotion Recognition System for e-learning improvement based on learner Concentric metric, International Conference on Computational Modeling and Security (CMS 2016), Procedia Computer Science 85 (2016) 767 – 776.

[2] https://www.academia.edu/40225184/Human_Face_Detection_and_Emotion_Recognition_u sing_Neural_Network. A Journal of TUTA, Pashchimanchal Campus, 05, 72-76

[3] Noesgaard S. S. and Ørngreen R. The Effectiveness of E-Learning: An Explorative and Integrative Review of the Definitions, Methodologies and Factors that Promote e-Learning Effectiveness" the Electronic Journal of eLearning Volume 13 Issue 4 2015, (pp278-290)

[4] O. El Hammoumi, F. Benmarrakchi, N. Ouherrou, J. El Kafi and A. El Hore, "Emotion Recognition in E-learning Systems," *2018 6th International Conference on Multimedia Computing and Systems (ICMCS)*, Rabat, 2018, pp. 1-6, doi: 10.1109/ICMCS.2018.8525872.

[5]https://www.verywellmind.com/understand-body-language-and-facial-expressions-4147228. [Retrieved at 2020 September 08].

[6] https://covid19.mohp.gov.np/ [Data retrieved at 2020 September 08].

[7] A. Gunasekaran, Ronald D. McNeil, Dennis shaul, E-learning research and applications, Industrial and Commercial Training, April 2002.

[8] Ayvaz, Ugur, Hüseyin Gurgler and Mehmet Osman Devrim. "USE OF FACIAL EMOTION RECOGNITION IN E-LEARNING SYSTEMS." *Information Technologies and Learning Tools* 60 (2017): 95-104.

[9]https://pathshalanepal.com/list-of-universities-in-nepal/ [Retrieved at 2020 September 08].

[10]https://www.kaggle.com/selfishgene/youtube-faces-with-facial-keypoints. [Retrieved at 2020 September 08].

[11]https://www.who.int/publications/m/item/draft-landscape-of-covid-19-candidate-vaccines. [Retrieved at 2020 September 08].

[12] Jithendran A., Pranav Karthik P., Santhosh S., Naren J. (2020) Emotion Recognition on E-Learning Community to Improve the Learning Outcomes Using Machine Learning Concepts: A Pilot Study. In: Somani A., Shekhawat R., Mundra A., Srivastava S., Verma V. (eds) Smart Systems and IoT: Innovations in Computing. Smart Innovation, Systems and Technologies, vol 141. Springer,Singapore.

YOUR KNOWLEDGE HAS VALUE

- We will publish your bachelor's and
  master's thesis, essays and papers

- Your own eBook and book -
  sold worldwide in all relevant shops

- Earn money with each sale

Upload your text at www.GRIN.com
and publish for free